AERIAL FLOW YOGA

AERIAL FLOW YOGA

AUTHORED BY
DEBOSHREE ROY

PENMAN BOOKS
A BOOK PUBLISHING COMPANY

PENMAN BOOKS

Office No. 303, Kumar House Building,
D Block, Central Market, Opp PVR Cinema,
Prashant Vihar, Delhi 110085, India
Website: www.penmanbooks.com
Email: publish@penmanbooks.com

First Published by Penman Books 2021

Title: Aerial Flow Yoga
Price: ₹599 | $ 10
ISBN: 978-93-90156-90-0

Dedication

I dedicate this book to my Father, Taposh Roy Chowdhury, whose name means Tapasya. Your willpower and love will forever inspire me. Thank you for being you baba.

I give special thanks and homage to my guide, mentor and teacher- Omprakash Gaur, without whom I would not have even started the journey of aerial yoga. You have been my guiding light and believed in me even when I couldn't see it myself. Thank you for everything and more.

And most of all, deepest gratitude and love for Gilroy D'Souza who has been my rock and my anchor, the one who has playfully taught me the value of principles, discipline and consistency. I stand tall only because you stand beside me. Thank you for being in my life and blessing me with your love.

Last but not the least, special mention to all my aerial students, who have stood by me and chosen to take this magical journey with me. You have made everything worth it.

Contents

But First

Before I begin this book, I just want to say this one thing: DON'T FREAK OUT! Don't freak out looking at some of the postures and do not take your mind to the place where it begins to say: Oh! I can never do that! Before your thoughts get there, stay with me awhile while I share a story with you. I promise to keep it short and sweet.

Once upon a time, there was a little girl who loved dancing. She would dance anywhere and everywhere. She would dance in the bathroom for hours with no one knowing. This little girl loved everything about moving, yet she never had any early exposure to any movement-related activities or classes. So the bathroom mirror remained her ever faithful companion for days, months and eventually years. This same girl lost her mother to Oral Cancer at the age of 10 which left her feeling quite bereft and lonely. In this time, for the first time in her life, she got a fit (A fit can be a brief moment when the person appears to be "absent" from what is going on around him or her, or jerking/twitching of a hand, arm or leg or jerking/twitching affecting the whole body. The patient may or may not become unconscious) where she lost consciousness for a short duration. She was misdiagnosed with Epilepsy and was from there on, treated with a very heavy dose of medication for the next few years. During this time, she put on a LOT of weight. She lost her appetite. She would always be sleepy. She lost bladder control. She started hallucinating; a scary man in white to be precise. She started to stammer. Her once beautiful handwriting, turned into a bundle of ants walking haphazardly on a sheet of paper. She lost confidence and the ability to look into people's eyes.

This same girl had a series of misfortunes during her schooling years which led to further mental trauma. So the little girl dancing in the bathroom was lost somewhere. Lost in pain. Lost in trauma. The little girl turned into a little lady aged 19. Fast forward to her college years, she opted for a girls' college for her confidence had taken a serious blow in her schooling years. During a lazy afternoon at the college canteen, she and 3 other girls decided to join a dance class. She was excited. She was nervous. But she really wanted to try. So she did. She ended up dancing center stage in that workshop. The little girl wasn't lost after all. The little lady went on to fully become a dancer and pursue a career in dancing. She found "home" in dancing. She found a place where she could express herself and just be herself. This same lady tried Aerial for the first time during her training years with a professional company based in Goa. She sucked. She had never ever in her life climbed or done anything remotely physical. Just her dancing since the age of 19. Everyone around her was trying flips, turns and falls from the air while she struggled to even climb the fabric once. But the little lady was persistent. Life had thrown many obstacles on her path and somehow she had managed to persevere. So she did what she did best. She worked harder than anyone else in the room. She came in first and left last.

And today, the same little lady shares her aerial world with you through this book. Yes, it's my story!

The little girl and the little lady made it; alive and thriving.

She just wants to tell you that if she can do it, then so can you!

So, keep the little girl/little boy inside you alive.

YOUR DREAMS MATTER!

Chapter One

What is the Meaning of Aerial and What is Aerial Flow Yoga?

The word "aerial" in itself signifies being airborne or existing, happening or operating in air. Aerial Flow Yoga is a unique combination of Yoga with Aerial arts. It has its roots in aerial silk, an acrobatic form of training the body by learning how to maneuver your body on a long piece of fabric. It requires precise training, tremendous strength, practice and coordination to become an Aerial Silk acrobat. With Aerial Flow Yoga, we take that same long fabric and change its shape into a U-shaped fabric and simply due to the change in its shape, a whole new world appears. A world where the marriage of Aerial arts and Yoga begins. To say that it is beautiful would only be apt. In this book, we combine the world of Hatha Yoga and Aerial Arts to form Aerial Flow Yoga, a form of practice that strengthens the body, challenges the mind and gives a tremendous sense of fulfillment to the practitioner. Because here is the truth; when we see pictures and visuals of someone doing Aerial Yoga, many of us would think I could never do that. This book is meant to change that thought. It's meant to show that with technique, guidance and a supportive learning atmosphere, 'I could never do that' can turn into 'I'm sure I can do that' and then some more.

By understanding the nuances of technique, Aerial Flow becomes not just a challenge for the body but also a doorway to connect with your fears and playfully transform them into wins. When we tick off something from our list that we think we could never do, it actually leads to the birth of authentic confidence. A confidence that has stemmed from your own body and not from some outside element. It is your moment of achievement and such moments are what bring you closer to authentic happiness. *Always remember, sound technique removes fear and technique applied makes you fearless.* This book is meant to help you start your aerial journey and bring out the aerial god/goddess inside you for once you achieve that fluidity in air, there is absolutely nothing that can parallel that feeling. It's like being on a high of freedom and strength which is achieved through your body and your will to grow. Yes, it's an unbeatable feeling! On this note, let's get started!

Chapter Two

Aerial Practice Checklist

There are a few things that you must be aware of before diving fully into an aerial practice-

Is my rig (practice space) safe?

Get your training spot checked for its weight-bearing capacity by a structural engineer. No one wants to have a face plant in the middle of a beautiful airborne moment. Also, always have a crash mat or a thick safety mat if you are trying something tricky. Even if you are confident about the trick/skill, don't risk injury by training without a safety mat.

Background in training

This is very crucial for a safe and healthy practice. What is the level of your training? If you are a complete beginner, it would be advisable to join aerial classes near you and try the flows mentioned in the book under the guidance of professionals only.

Preparation before actual aerial work

This one is a very important question for anyone who wants a long life of training and wants to reduce the chances of injury during training. The floor is your best teacher. Always have a great flow/stretching/conditioning routine of at least 30-40 mins set out for yourself if you are a complete beginner. 25 mins if you are more advanced in your practice. Make sure that you have warmed up very well and make a routine that combines stretching with strengthening and core work. The balance is crucial in aerial to avoid chances of injury. Special focus should be on shoulder opening and shoulder conditioning as you need a lot of upper body strength for doing aerial. Trust me, your future self will really thank you for this.

Training with someone around you

If you are fairly well acquainted with the hammock and feel confident to train on your own, that's great but not under my watch! Have a friend or family member with you/

around you whenever you try something new. Trust me, nothing is worth the unforeseen injury!

Extremities training

A lot of us get excited about getting the fancy stuff on the hammock while completely ignoring the extremities of our bodies, I mean our fingers and our feet. Basically, no matter how beautifully you color the inside of a shape, if the color is leaking out from the sides, the picture isn't going to look the way you want it to. Work on training your feet so that your body understands what it means to keep the entire length of your leg active while in the air. It starts from your feet. You can try the exercise- Point flex + kick-ups mentioned in Chapter 7 - Aerial Hammock Conditioning.

Chapter Three
Frequently Used Terms

Before we dive headlong into the guide, there are some terms that you would come across repeatedly while thumbing through the book. Here is an explanation of those terms-

Inverted Stag

Inverted stag is an ending position and a transition pose for many flows/sequences on the hammock. It is used for completing many different sequences that you will find out ahead. To find stability in those poses, it is crucial to have a very strong knee clip (intensity of grabbing the fabric from the back of the knee).

Sirsasana (Headstand)

Sirsasana is a starting pose and a transition pose in our aerial world. There is also a term called Double Sirsasana which simply means Sirsasana done twice. There is a traditional Yoga version and an aerial version. For the aerial version, always ensure that the fabric is placed correctly, supporting the sacrum.

Dandasana (Staff pose)

Dandasana is a transition pose in the aerial world. It is sometimes used as a resting pose in the middle of a challenging flow. There is a traditional way in Yoga of performing Dandasana on the mat and an Aerial version of performing it on the hammock.

Upavistha Konasana (Wide-angled extended leg stretch)

Upavistha Konasana is a transition pose for many sequences throughout the book. For a clean posture, ensure that the back of the knees are straight and the feet are pointed.

Note: There is sometimes a confusion between Upavishthakonasana and Straddle. Note that Upavishthakonasana is also a wide-legged position as is Straddle. The difference lies in the fact that Upavishthakonasana is when you are sitting upright on the hammock and Straddle is when you are inverted (upside-down)

Straddle (Inversion)

Straddle is a term that comes from the Aerial world. It is also a transition pose that is used to define the position of being inverted in the air with both legs open and feet pointed. It challenges your grip strength, your core strength and overall body conditioning. It is crucial to understand the importance of a straddle as it defines your progress as you keep advancing in your aerial journey. A lot of advance drops require a clean straddle to transition to the next step of preparation.

Note: Both images shown below are that of straddles. The first one requires grip strength and core stability as there is no support of the hammock on the lower back. However, the second one is relatively easier as the fabric is supporting the lower back and all that needs to be kept in mind is the lengthening of the back of the knees and the inner thighs touching the hammock.

Chapter Four
Standing Warm-Up Poses

To start an aerial flow hammock class, it is best to use the hammock to open the shoulders, warm-up the hamstrings and engage the core slightly to ensure better results through the class. The hammock can be used in a multitude of creative ways to help you make your warm up sequence extremely creative and flowy. These standing poses are fun, interesting and extremely doable once you have the technique nailed. *Always remember, sound technique removes fear and technique applied makes you fearless.* So let's break it down further to make it easier to understand. Here we go –

Warm-Up Exercises

1. Chest Expansion Exercises
2. Wrist Lock Forward Bend
3. Lateral Spinal Twists + Lateral Stretch with Hammock

Standing Poses

1. Trikonasana (Triangle pose)
2. Prasarita Padottanasana (Extended wide-legged stretch)
3. Virabhadrasana (Warrior 3)
4. Navasana (Boat pose)
5. Uttanasana (Intense forward bend stretch)

Warm-Up Exercises Explained

1. Chest Expansion Exercises: This is a great way to start a class by opening up the chest, stretching the shoulders and allowing the breathing to go deeper. You can start the sequence by bringing the hammock under your shoulder blades. Make sure you spread out the fabric so it doesn't dig too much into your skin. On the inhale, interlace your fingers above your head and expand the chest while pushing the pelvis forward and keeping the chin tucked in. Breathing better is the primary aim in Yoga and what better way to start than at the very beginning of the class. Deep belly-breathing or "balloon breathing" could be an ideal term. Expand the belly while inhaling and contract while exhaling. Allow this awareness to remain with you throughout your practice. So much so that it becomes like second nature to you.

From there, exhale to come back to a sitting position with knees bent and arms wrapping around each other & inhale to expand into the stretch again. Hold the pose for at least 3 deep breaths and repeat 3-4 times.

2. Wrist Lock Forward Bend: This one is another great shoulder opener. It would be great to try this stretch as much as your flexibility permits. To begin, take your hands outside the hammock and join your palms. Then rotate the wrists to bring your hands inside the hammock to create a lock around them. Then inhale and as you exhale, slide into a forward bend. If you have tight glutes /hamstrings or tightness in your lower back, you can keep your knees slightly bent but keep the tummy tucked in and with every exhalation, try to bring the chest closer and closer towards the mat. Keep the entire length of your arms alive and active, keeping the elbows straight and fingers active. Make sure you relax the neck and jaw and don't hold any unnecessary tension while doing the pose. Your shoulder blades will say a sweet thank you after you come out of it. Inhale to come out of it, back into a standing position and exhale to go into it again. Repeat 3 times. Make sure that you don't shift your weight forward from your legs and are firmly rooted into the floor with only the upper body sliding forward and coming back to a neutral standing position.

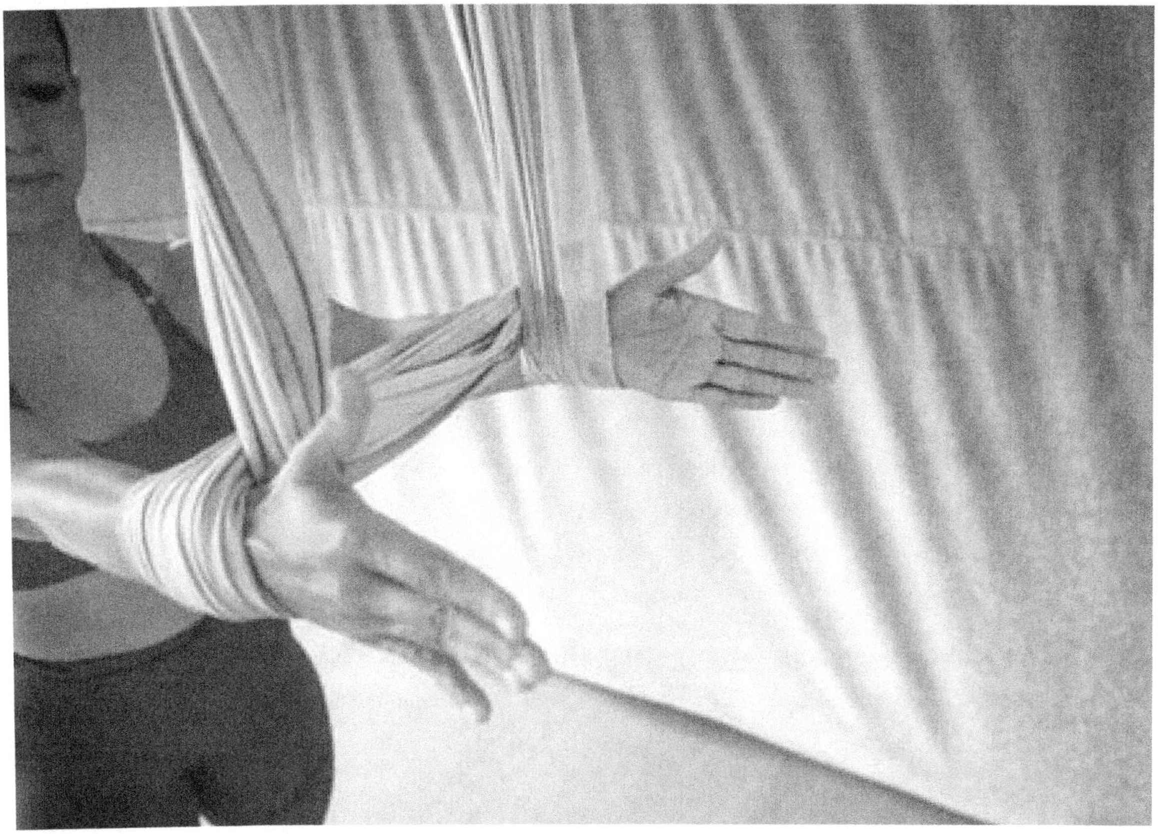

3. Lateral Spinal Twists + Lateral Stretch with Hammock: Lateral means "Sideways" and in this case, it would mean a sideways stretch with the help of the hammock. It is another wonderful warm-up exercise. Start by standing behind the hammock in Tadasana. Spread out your toes, pull up the knee-caps, activate mula bandha (A Sanskrit term **meaning** "root lock", **mula bandha** is the yogic practice of drawing the root chakra up and in. The root chakra is said to be located at the base of the torso, or the perineum, which is the area between your anus and genitals). Then hold the hammock in front of you and take your arms all the way over your head with your face between your arms. Inhale and lift the rib cage, press your shoulders down and exhale to twist towards your right side. Make sure the pelvis is neutral and both hip points are front-facing as you try this twist. Keep breathing well as you go through it. Inhale to come the center and exhale to twist on either side. Repeat 2 times. To go into a lateral spinal stretch, keep the hammock overhead and then front-facing, simply lean onto your left side with your entire torso. Keep the arms and shoulder-width apart, elbows straight and make sure that the hip points are still facing the front. Repeat the same on the right side and do this 2 times on each side.

Standing Warm-Up Poses

1. Trikonasana: Also known as the triangle pose, this is great for a deep oblique stretch and hip opening. For this asana as a warm-up, try not to focus too much on pushing the stretch but rather allowing the breathing to go deeper and gently push the hips forward in every exhalation. To get into it, come into a profile position with your right shoulder facing the hammock. Make a T-shape with your feet with your left foot facing away and the right foot parallel to the hammock.

From there, take your left leg forward, right leg back (minimum gap between the legs being the length of your leg). Maintaining this position, lift your right hand and wrap your arm around the fabric twice. Inhale, pull up the rib cage, bring the left arm in the same line as your shoulders and then exhale to drop to your left side trying to make sure that the right heel, hip and shoulder all remain in the same line. You can also use a block for support if needed. Hold the pose for at least 10 breaths and then repeat on the other side. And yes, don't forget to breathe!

Benefits

This pose helps in stretching the hips, back muscles, chest and shoulders. Stretches the spine. Gives Strength to the thighs, calves and glutes. Stimulates the spinal nerves. Improves spinal flexibility, helps in the correct alignment of the shoulders. Helps in relieving backache, gastritis, indigestion, acidity & flatulence. Assists in the treatment of neck sprains, reduces stiffness in the neck, shoulders and knees, strengthens the ankles and tones the ligaments of the arms and legs. It also stimulates the nervous system and alleviates nervous depression, strengthens the pelvic area and tones the reproductive organs.

Focusing Chakra

- Heart Chakra (Anahata Chakra)
- Sacral Chakra (Swadisthana Chakra)
- Root Chakra (Muladhara Chakra)

Tips

- Elbows straight and not bent
- Active legs with toes spread out
- Knee-caps pulled up
- Glutes Active & engaged

2. Prasarita Padottanasana-Standing Wide-Legged Forward Bend With Hammock: This one is a beautiful pose for opening up those hamstrings, glutes and shoulders. To get into it, create a wrist lock again by keeping the arms and shoulder-width apart and make sure that the fingers are open and active, palms facing each other. Bring your legs into a wide-legged position, slightly wider than your hip-width but not too wide at the same time. Breathe in and as you breathe out, slide into a forward bend. Make sure that the elbows are lengthening and keep tucking the belly in as you exhale while pushing the chest out towards the mat in every exhalation. I basically mean, relax deep into it. The more you relax and breathe into it, the more naturally the chest will surrender towards the mat. This is a great warm-up for opening up the shoulders and warming up the hamstrings before the Sun Salutation Series. Keep the knees bent if you have had any history of back pain or injury.

Benefits

This pose stretches the backs of the legs – Hamstrings, calves, glutes and lower back. It improves hip-joint flexibility and strengthens the feet. It acts as a semi inversion and creates length in the spine. Improves posture and provides rest to the heart. If done on the hammock, this pose also helps in opening the shoulders and preparing the body for the next part of the class.

Focusing Chakras

- Crown Chakra (Sahasrara Chakra)
- Third Eye Chakra (Ajna Chakra)
- Solar Plexus (Manipura Chakra)
- Sacral Chakra (Swadisthana Chakra)
- Root Chakra (Muladhara Chakra)

Tips:

- Make sure that the elbows are straight
- Back of the knees extended (bent in case of previous back injury or lower back discomfort)
- Chest pushing towards the mat, aiming to get it parallel with your mat
- Weight slightly on the front of the toes

3. Virabhadrasana 3/Warrior 3: This one is one of my absolute favorites. Why? Because it really brings out the inner warrior! Activating all the muscles in your legs, shoulders and core, this one calls for complete awareness and attention! It is absolutely amazing for strengthening your legs, glutes, core and lower back muscles. It is great for spinal alignment and in general, does exactly what it says. Makes you a warrior. For this pose, we can hold the hammock in 2 ways, depending on what feels comfortable and doesn't strain the lower back more than it should. The first way is to again rest the hands inside the hammock, shoulder-width apart and keep the fingers active. The second way is to come into a wrist lock to ensure more stability. To get into the pose, once you have stabilized your hands inside the hammock, breathe in and as you breathe out, slide the upper torso forward and lift the right leg up to 90 degrees with the hip closed and foot flexed. Imagine your body as one block, moving together in harmony as opposed to two separate chunks with the torso and the leg moving separately. It is important to ensure that the standing leg is strong and the toes are spread out to help in activating the calf muscles and the length of the entire thigh and glutes. Feel the burn, revel in it, don't allow the back to arch and you are definitely doing a great job! Hold for 5-8 deep breaths, release to come back to a standing position and then change sides.

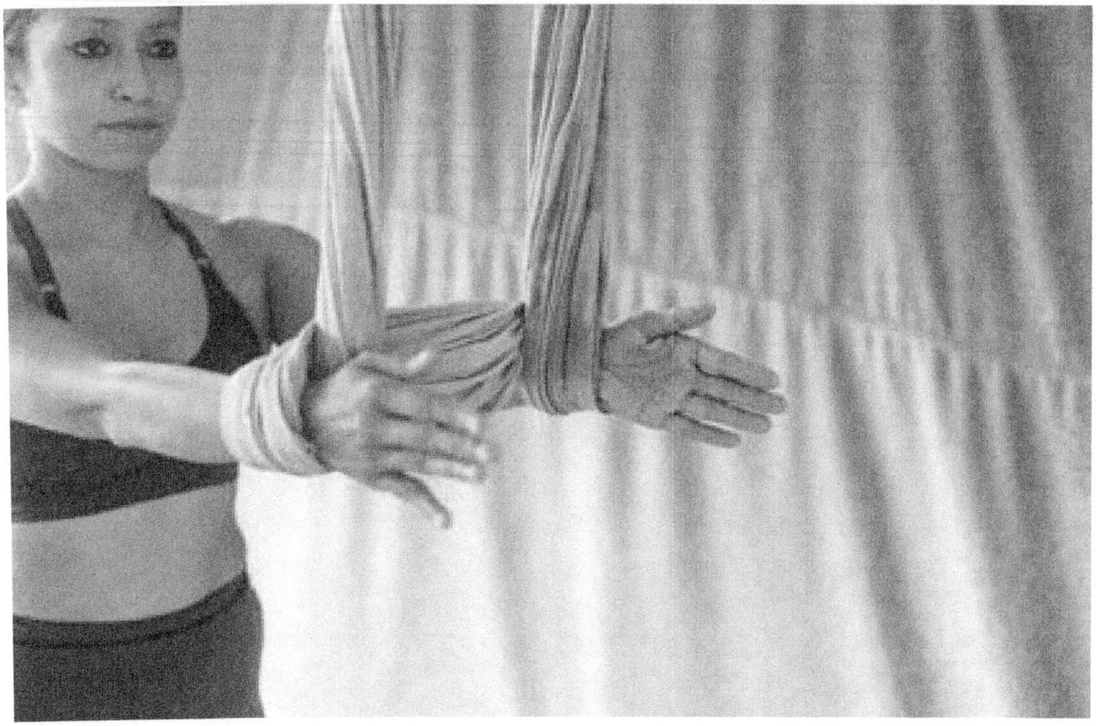

Benefits

- Strengthens the whole back side of the body, including the shoulders, hamstrings, calves and ankles.
- Tones and strengthens the abdominal muscles
- Improves balance, posture, and full-body coordination

Focusing Chakra

- Solar Plexus (Manipura Chakra)
- Sacral Chakra (Swadisthana Chakra)
- Root Chakra (Muladhara Chakra)

Tips

- Keep the standing leg extremely strong with the toes spread out
- Bring awareness to the lower back so it is not arching
- Abdomen tucked in
- Keep the raised leg in line with your torso.
- Keep the breathing going!

4. Naukasana With Hammock: This pose is great for strengthening the lower back and the spinal extensors. It is excellent for people with lower back issues or people who have stiffness/ discomfort arising out of bad posture. To practice Naukasana, push the hammock down with your fingers pushing it down as you go on the tip of your toes. Make sure your thumbs are more apart than the hip-width to ensure that the thumbs don't get stuck as you lean forward. Lean forward and as soon as you feel the hammock taking your entire weight, lift the legs off the floor, adjust your fingers, allowing them to slide up and you come into Naukasana! Now change the grip of your hands, one hand at a time with the thumbs facing up and make sure that the elbows remain straight.

This will cause an outward rotation of the shoulder blades which is exactly what we are aiming for. Roll the shoulders back to enable more chest expansion. Make sure that the curve of the body is maintained with the upper body and lower body lengthening and the knees are straight. For some fun, you can try this warm-up with a swing. Just take a few steps back with the hammock. Lean forward and the moment you put your weight into the hammock and lift the legs, you will go into flying Naukasana.

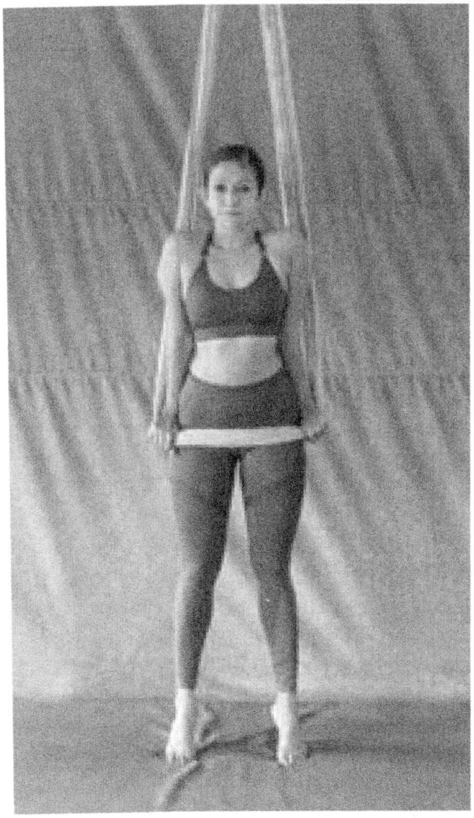

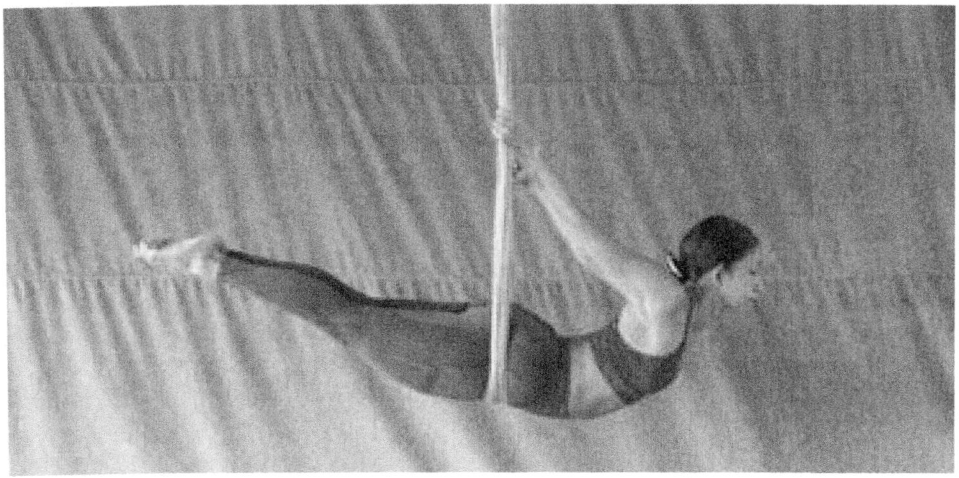

Benefits

Conditions the abdominal muscles, spinal column and spinal muscles. Enhances digestion and improves posture by shoulder opening.

Focusing Chakra

- ANAHATA (Heart Chakra)

Tips

- Keep both feet together to ensure glute activation
- Create a lovely curved straight line with the upper body and lower body following the same line

5. Uttanasana: The pose opens up the chest, thereby improving the lung capacity. It elongates the spine, decreasing the chances of osteoporosis and promotes a healthy neurological system, thus preventing high blood pressure. To practice Uttanasana on the hammock, place both hands on either side of the hammock. Make sure that the fingers are more apart than the hip-width or the thumbs might get stuck during the forward bend. Go on the tip of your toes and lean forward while maintaining the position of the hammock under the hip bone. Allow the belt to take the entire weight of the body while the toes remain touching the ground. They don't necessarily have to touch the floor completely as the heels might slightly come off the floor. You can keep blocks under your feet if you feel that your feet go completely off the floor. Make sure that you don't feel a lot of weight on your arms and you surrender completely into the hammock. Go into deep belly-breathing and you would enjoy the deep benefits of this posture. To get into the VARIATION of Uttanasana, lift both legs off the mat, making sure that there is ample gap between the legs and the back of the knees are straight with the feet pointed. Try to ensure that the legs don't drop down towards the mat. Imagine your body being almost as straight as an arrow. Just diagonally! Keep pressing the mat away to go deeper into this stretch by lengthening the spine and then clip both your feet from the outside of the hammock. It's okay for the back to arch in this position. To come out of the pose, simply place one leg at a time back on the mat and then curve the spine to come up slowly. Make sure to keep the chin tucked in for a few moments to avoid dizziness.

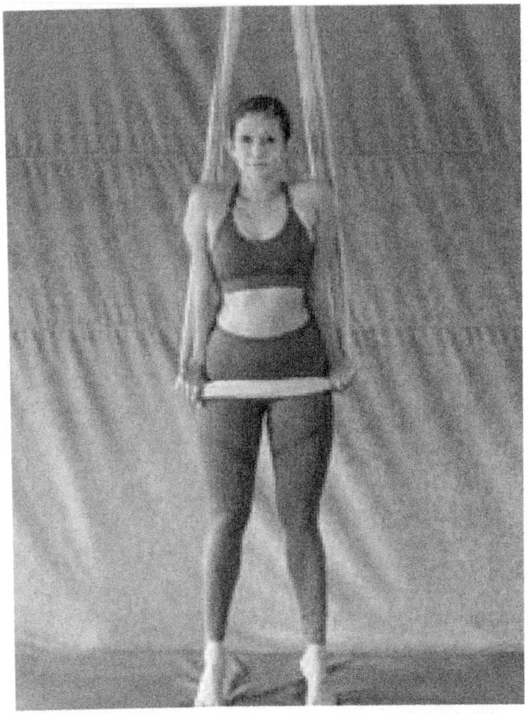

Benefits

- Strengthens the core muscles
- Massages and tones the kidney & liver
- Helps in better functioning of lungs because of chest expansion
- Opens the hip flexors and relieves tension/tightness in the groin

Focusing Chakra

- Ajna Chakra (Third Eye)

Tips

- Keep the legs wide apart and take them up and away from each other
- Keep the elbows straight to ensure that you are not putting undue stress on your shoulders
- Keep the feet pointed and extend the back of the knees
- Fingers remain active in the variation

"

Studio Naach Stories

If we can do it, so can you

Medha Monteneiro is an artist based in Goa who loves to fly. She started her aerial journey at age of 55. She is an inspiration to one and all around her because of her fearlessness and her attitude towards her body and life. She has become adept at helping complete beginners and inspiring everyone to start their aerial journey from a place of joy and not fear. A round of applause for Medha please!

"

Chapter Five

Surya Namaskar Floor-Warm-Up

We use Surya Namaskar (Sun Salutation) as a warm-up on the floor to get our body ready for aerial. A Surya Namaskar is essentially a series of 12 asanas in which movement and breath find coordination. Each movement has a corresponding way to breathe along with it, ensuring all the help needed from our method of breathing to better perform the pose. We start the class with this because what better way to start than to create harmony between our breathing and movement. I, personally, have gone into deep meditative states after performing 40-100 Surya Namaskars. Thought ceases to exist and you become one with the breath. Only the present moment and its completeness remain, shedding away everything else unnecessary. For your self-practice, you can choose to do as many repetitions as you please. For our aerial class, we choose 6 Surya Namaskars with the last 2 having different variations. You can keep playing with the variations to open up different parts of your body. Let's dive into this harmonious series as old as time and as precious as the sun we salute!

You can start your Surya Namaskar practice by standing in **Samasthiti** (Equal Standing) is a command to attention, to stand in balanced stillness. It is the practice of standing with equal, steady, and still attention.). Become aware of your breath, take a few moments to quieten the thoughts and be present with your body. To begin-

- Inhale to go into Urdhva Hastasana
- Exhale to go into Padahastasana-Inhale to go into Ashwa Sanchalanasana
- Hold your breath in Kumbhakasana
- Exhale to Ashtanga Pranam with knees, chest and forehead to the floor
- Inhale to Bhujangasana
- Exhale to come into Parvatasana
- Inhale to come back to Ashwa Sanchalanasana
- Exhale to come back to Padahastasana
- Inhale to come back to Urdhva Hastasana

Relax for a few breaths in Samasthiti and carry on with the repetitions.

URDHVA HASTASANA
(Upward salute)
INHALE

PADAHASTASANA
(Hand to foot forward bend)
EXHALE

ASHWA
SANCHALANASANA
(Equestrian Pose)
INHALE

KUMBHAKASANA
(Plank Pose)
RETAIN YOUR BREATH

ASHTANGA PRANAM
(Knee chest forehead pose)
EXHALE

BHUJANGASANA
(Cobra Pose)
INHALE

PARVATASANA
(Mountain Pose)
EXHALE

ASHWASANCHALANASANA
(Equestrian Pose)
INHALE

PADAHASTASANA
(Hand to foot forward bend)
EXHALE

URDHVA HASTASANA
(Upward Salute Pose)
INHALE

Chapter Six

Standing Moving Series

We now come to the moving series with the hammock. Again, all through these exercises, put all your attention into coordinating your breath with your movement. At the end of the day, all of this movement is for the sole purpose of finding stillness within and a sense of harmony with your breath. The series that we will tackle here can have various progressions ranging from beginners to advanced practice. Let's get started!

1. The Movement Series
2. The Lunge Series
3. The Warrior 3 Series

1. The Movement Series: The movement series are designed to work the hip flexors and help stretch them. It will work your core, help you get better with coordination and develop more stability & flexibility in your shoulders.

We start the series by standing behind the hammock. Lift your right leg and insert the right foot inside the hammock, making sure that the hammock is supporting the ankle completely. To awaken the ankle muscles and the length of the entire leg, we first go into a series of points and flex with our toes. Keeping the arms shoulder level, ensure that the bottom leg is firmly grounded on the floor. The standing leg's foot should be completely parallel to the mat with the toes spread out evenly to ensure that the calves, thighs and glutes remain active and engaged. Your standing leg gives you the strength for the working leg to move freely (and be awesome). In case of difficulty in free movement of the leg inside the hammock due to tight hip flexors, it would be best recommended to reduce the height of the hammock to a more comfortable height or keep the knee bent for the first few attempts. For the next step, we maintain our arms shoulder level, keeping the gaze fixed on the horizon, focus on the breath and reaching out with our fingertips to make sure that the chest remains open and the spine long.

Inhale, we move our right leg to the right side. Keep the right foot pointed throughout. Exhale, we bring the leg back in center. Repeat this series about 4 times and each time you exhale, try to ensure the full range of motion with the leg inside the hammock. It's okay if you lose balance in the beginning! Rome wasn't built in a day. So give your body the gift of patience and practice. For the next step, we flex our foot inside the hammock and keep it flexed throughout the practice. Grab the hammock with both hands. Cross the fabrics creating a more stable hold for your foot inside the hammock. Make sure that the shoulders are rolled back to avoid any hunching. Inhale and grab the hammock and expand the chest, while exhaling we go deep into a forward bend or Padangusthasana with the hammock support. Make sure that elbows are pointing outwards and it is better to initiate the movement from the chest and not the head during any forward bend. The aim is not to touch the head to the thigh but the chest to the thigh which comes when we originate the movement from the lower spine. Repeat this 3 times and on the 4th exhalation, hold the position longer and go deep into your breathing. Keep the foot flexed and in every exhalation try to get the chest closer to the thigh without allowing tension to pervade into your neck and jaw.

For the next step, hold both strands of the fabric in your right hand, open your left arm and left foot towards the left side with the movement originating from the base leg. Once you are facing the left side inhale, lift up your left arm and bring it right next to your left ear. Exhale to stretch laterally to grab the hammock. Ensure that both the elbows are straight and use your top hand to twist your chest open even more by pushing the hammock away and go deeper into your obliques. If you wish to go into a deeper stretch, you can simply slide your hands lower along the hammock, come to grab your right fabric with both your hands and twist the chest to open more while the foot rests on the hammock. Yes, that divine feeling when you open your chest is unbeatable! For the next step, inhale and bring both the arms right next to your ears, completely parallel to each other and laser straight. No bent elbows wanted here!

Exhale and start turning the entire body to the opposite side by using the base leg to help you turn and keeping the torso upright. You want to bend the knee inside the hammock, so much so, that the heel should touch your glutes. Then take a hop if you need to and adjust yourself to bring the body right under the hammock because for the next step, you would need to be in line with the hammock or the body will slide either to the right or the left. Slide your hands up the hammock till the elbows become completely straight. Your thumbs should be facing up. Inhale, bend the front knee and then slide all the way back using the leg inside the hammock. We call this the SLIDING NATARAJASANA. Exhale, come back up to the standing position. Repeat this process about 3 times and then on the 4th exhalation, try to hold the position for as long as you can while you keep the breathing even.

Attempt to straighten the front and back knee completely. If you are a beginner, you don't have to attempt this. Think more of alignment and breath awareness. Keep the left foot pressing the ground firmly to ensure that the body remains stable. Come back to the starting position and you are good to go into Natarajasana which would be the final position for this series. The entire series has prepared you for this final pose which is also called the dancer's pose. Because this pose uses muscles from all over the body, it is known to restore a sense of invigoration and power after you have held it for some time.

To go into Natarjasana using the hammock, cross the strands of the hammock to ensure more stability. Your thumbs are again facing down. Now, keeping the gaze fixed and the breathing even, lift the leg and try the first variation with the chest while leaning forward. Then

come back to a neutral position and try the final variation where you don't allow the chest to fall forward. Pull the fabric to take the leg higher and keep the chest expanded and upright. Consciously communicate with your body while holding this pose to allow more freedom in the shoulders, lower back and glutes. After holding it with even breathing for about 5-6 breaths, gently release the foot with control and slide the foot out and repeat the entire process on the left side. And yes, don't forget to applaud your efforts! You did very well!

Tips

- All through the series, keep the extremities of the body alive (toes and fingertips)
- Keep the standing leg strong throughout your practice
- Make sure the thumbs are facing up in your grip while trying the Natarajasana

2. The Lunge Series: The lunge series uses the hammock to play with variations of Ashwa Sanchalanasana, Kumbhakasana and Hanumanasana. Depending on the level of your practice, you can try a more challenging or easier version of the pose. All that is important is listening to where your body is and pushing accordingly. This practice is for your growth and happiness. Never let this slip your mind.

We start the Lunge series by going into a mountain pose on the mat, making sure that the hammock is behind our legs. From there, you can raise the right leg in the air and insert it inside the hammock. Your ankle should be resting on the fabric. Keep the feet either pointed or flexed to ensure that the leg remains active and engaged. I prefer to keep the feet flexed and leave it that way throughout the series. After placing the right foot inside, walk back with your hands as you bend the left knee. Walk back with the hands till the hands rest on either side of your feet. Once you reach this position, ideally your chest should be kissing your thigh and keep the gaze slightly upward to maintain the line of the spine. It is of key importance to keep the back of the knee straight for the leg inside the hammock. To carry on, we take a deep inhalation, twist our torso towards the right side and raise our right arm next to our ears. Exhale and bring it back to the same position next to your foot. We do the same on the left side. Repeat this movement 2 more times. Now, fix your gaze on any object slightly ahead of you. Inhale and as you exhale, take both arms off the ground while keeping the left knee still bent and the arms at shoulder level. Ensure that the knee doesn't cross the line of your ankle. Try to hold the pose for at least 3 deep breaths while maintaining stability and engagement throughout the body. After that, come back down and place both your hands again on each side of the right foot. Gently start sliding the back leg further back to slide into Hanumanasana. Go only till the lengths you feel comfortable and hold it for 4-5 deep breaths for the stretch to go deep. Come back from the Hanumanasana by walking forward with your hands again. Then take both your feet inside the hammock so that you are in a plank (Kumbhakasana) position. Ensure that the back is not arching, the glutes are active and the abdominal muscles are engaged, keeping the entire body in one line and the head in line with the spine.

Before we start with the left side, we practice knee-tucks. Yes, it is not easy. And yes, nothing easy EVER made you stronger. So let's get into it! As you are in the plank position and try the knee tuck variation, keep the feet pointed and back of the knees bent and then stack your glutes right on top of your shoulders, bringing your weight on your shoulders and arms. Make sure that the elbows are straight and you are firmly pushing the mat away. Inhale to come back to a neutral plank and exhale to come into a knee-tuck. After completing 5-6 knee-tucks, you can start the lunge series on the left side and give yourself a much-deserved round of applause after completing the full series! Increase or decrease the number of knee-tucks depending on how you are feeling. Sky's the limit!

Tips

- Make sure that you are breathing well throughout the practice
- You can bend the knee inside the hammock in case of tightness in the glutes
- In case of feeling weak in the middle of Kumbhakasana (plank), immediately take one leg out and rest on your mat. Yes, we don't need a face plant even at the cost of losing entertainment value in the class!

3. Warrior 3 Series: The warrior 3 in and of itself strengthens the entire length of the back of the body including the shoulders, hamstrings, calves, ankles, and back. It also tones and strengthens the abdominal muscles.

Warrior III improves balance, posture and full-body coordination. Once we modify it for the aerial version, there are a number of challenges that we can include depending on the level of our practice.

We begin the warrior 3 series by facing the hammock, inserting the right leg inside it and then turn to face the opposite side by rotating the base foot and bending the knee of the leg inside the hammock. We want to ensure that the base leg is completely straight and special emphasis is on spreading the toes evenly, keeping the kneecaps pulled up, the thighs and glutes active. Yes, I will keep repeating this till it becomes a mantra in your head and your body magically starts magically applying it through the habit of repetition! I want you to imagine that your leg is grounding on the earth through the entire series.

To begin, open your arms shoulder level and ensure that you can see your fingertips from the peripheral vision. Keep the chest expanded and the abdomen pulled up. With that in mind, we start a series of bending and straightening of the base leg. Keep the foot flexed inside the hammock and don't put too much pressure down with the ankle pressing down as this may lead to discomfort in the knee. Inhale and as you exhale, bend the base knee, keeping the knee inside the hammock bent as well and exhale to stretch and extend both knees. Move your arms in tune with the inhale and exhale to keep the flow of the series alive. Inhale, bring your arms at the shoulder level and exhale, bend your knees and bring your arms around yourself almost like you are hugging yourself (or kung fu panda, whichever makes the arms move with more energy!) Repeat this 4 times and in the 5th exhalation, keep both the knees bent, inhale and then extend the arms right next to the ears, bringing the palms together in Namaste position and exhale while twisting and forming the Namaste position of your hands. You want to ensure that once you are in the twist, the knee inside the hammock lengthens and the base knee remains bent without the knee over crossing the toes. Make sure that the palms are strongly pressing against each other which helps the top shoulder to open more towards the sky. Use the elbow to lock outside your knee to maintain a good twist. Hold the position for at least 5-6 deep breaths. From there, come back to a lunge again and then curve the entire length of your spine and even your head tucked in towards your chin to roll up (think of yourself as a snake!) and come to

a standing position. As you are in the standing position, you can bend the knee inside the hammock and take a few breaths to relax and allow the breathing to come back to neutral. Keep the eyes closed and all your attention on the air passing in and out of your nostrils or in the center of your forehead between the eyebrows. Once the breathing is equanimous again, take a deep breath, lift your arms up next to your ears and as you exhale, lean forward in a flat back position and place your left hand on the block placed right in front of the left leg. Bring the right arm right next to the ears and the palm should be facing inward. Keeping the elbows razor straight for both arms, deepen your breathing and hold the position for 5-6 breaths. If there is any form of discomfort in the lower back, you can bend the standing knee. If you wish to challenge yourself more, elevate the leg inside the hammock and free it from the hammock support while bringing both arms next to your ears and completing the full warrior 3.

Tips

- Make sure you are right on top of the standing leg and that your weight isn't shifting back as you hold the pose

- Your upper torso should be completely parallel to the floor in the final position and the glutes should be actively engaged
- Keep both arms parallel to the ears

"

Studio Naach Stories

If we can do it, so can you

Mansi is a chef and entrepreneur based in Goa. A mother of 4, she is relentless in her pursuit of physical fitness. She started her aerial journey at the age of 39 and continues to inspire us all with her multifaceted personality and her determination to keep fitness a priority in her life. Round of applause for Mansi!

"

Chapter Seven

Aerial Hammock Conditioning

What does conditioning mean and how does it help you in any form of practice? BODY CONDITIONING refers to exercises we do that add to our speed, endurance and overall physical ability of the body to try and execute challenging physical tasks. Be it in aerial or any other physical practice, conditioning is of key importance to get the results that you want. It ensures longevity of the body, understanding of what your body is naturally good at and what needs work and more than anything, if you have a challenging set of conditioning exercises, it will always help you in every aspect of your practice. To be fluid in air means a lot of groundwork for building a stable foundation to ensure that we have the strength and endurance needed while being airborne. Now let's get you started on that journey to get you stronger and definitely more able! Building upper body strength will be a challenging yet fun journey for many of you reading this book. Just remember that continued practice and dedication will definitely bring you on the path of awesomeness and all that you want to achieve in your aerial world! In conditioning, we break down the exercises to target different parts of the body. Be it the upper body, legs or core, there are a host of exercises that we can play with. So let's start playing!

These are few of the exercises that we begin with-

1. Hammock Pull-Ups (Building Shoulder Stability + Arm Strength)
2. Upside Down Crunches (Building Core Strength)
3. Point Flex Exercise + Kick Ups (Getting those beautiful leg extensions)
4. Knee Tucks (Building Lower Ab Strength)
5. Tabletop (Building Shoulder Stability & Core Strengthening)
6. Pull Up Bent Elbow Hold (Building Shoulder and Bicep Strength)
7. Straddle Back (Building Strength for inversions in Air)

1. Hammock Pull-Ups: For hammock pull-ups, sit in a dandasana pose on your mat right under the hammock. Lift your arms and take them outside and around the fabric. Make sure the wrists are turned inwards. Think of rotating your shoulders inwards. Maintain that alignment all through the pull-ups. Lean back and roll the shoulders back and push the chest slightly out. Press your feet into the ground with your heels and the feet flexed. Keep the big toes touching each other. Inhale to prepare and pull up on the exhale. Inhale, come back to a plank-position making sure that the glutes do not touch the mat. As you pull up, aim to get your chin almost to the same level as your hammock. Don't worry if you can't do this today! We will still be applauding your efforts and cheering for you on the day that you manage to do it! Do 2 sets of 5-10 reps depending on your endurance and desire to push yourself.

2. Upside Down Crunches: For this awesome set of crunches, you need to get into a sirsasana and slide both legs up the hammock. Make sure that the fabric is supporting your lower back, not your middle back and your inner thighs are squeezed well. Keeping that engagement alive, cross your hands over your chest or interlace your fingers behind your head and let's start the crunches! Think of your face touching your knees for the first 5 reps and the aim to touch your right toes with your left hand and left toes with your right hand. To challenge yourself even more, bring the upper torso parallel to the floor in an "L" position and try to hold for a minimum of 10 seconds. Repeat 3 sets of 10-15 reps and then come out slowly to avoid a spinning head. This set will definitely get your core burning and give you the strength you desire!

3. Point Flex Exercise + Kick-Ups: For this exercise, lie on your back. Bend both knees and place your feet hip width apart. From there, extend the right leg on the mat. Then lift it to 90 degrees with the feet pointed and back of the knee straight. We point and flex our right foot 10 times, followed by bringing the right leg down to go into a series of kick-ups with the left knee bent and foot still placed on the mat. Think of squeezing the inner thigh muscles really well as you go into the kicks. During the kick-ups, avoid any arch in the lower back and that can happen if you think of turning your pubic bone towards the abdomen, ensuring that there is no arch in your back while doing the kick-ups.

Do 2 sets of 10 reps for each leg. Repeat the same thing on the left side followed by ankle rotations with special attention to feet articulation. Yes, those calves will burn and that's what we want!

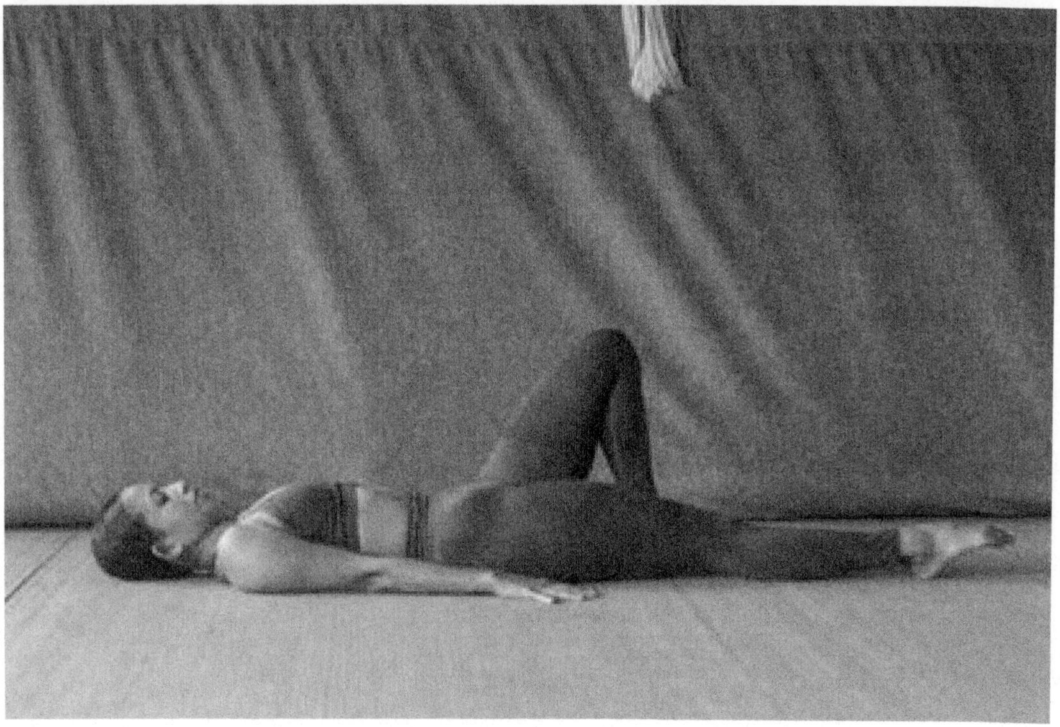

4. Knee-Tucks: For this exercise, make sure that your lats are warmed up very well. From a standing position, slide both your shoulders inside the hammock. Lift your arms up, making sure that the elbows are straight and the shoulders are rolled back. Wrap your arms around the fabric twice, make sure that the shoulders are inwardly rotated and the wrists are facing each other. Activate the shoulders and hang from the hammock by hugging your knees to your chest. In the inhale, bring the knees down and in the exhale, tuck the knees towards your chest again. Try to hold the knee-tuck position for 5 seconds in each rep and in the final rep of a round, hold the knees close to your chest for at least 15 seconds and then repeat 3 rounds of 10 reps each time. I know you may want to kill me as you do this but you will definitely love me when your inversions get better precisely because of this!

5. Tabletops: For table tops, come on all fours on your mat and from there slide one foot at a time inside the hammock to come into a full-plank (Kumbhakasana) position. Make sure that your back is not arching or the hips are not too high. For the correct tabletop position, you want to make sure that your hands remain rooted to the ground. Inhale in the plank position and as you exhale, lift your hips to neatly stack them right over your shoulders. If keeping the knees straight is challenging in the beginning, try it with bent knees and from there, work up till the knees are completely straight. Ensure that your elbows are straight, you are pushing the mat away and the feet are pointed. Come back to a neutral plank and then come back to a tabletop from there. Repeat 2 sets of 10 reps.

Variation

For a more challenging variation, come into tabletop and from there, you can try to lift one leg off the hammock, coming into a half-handstand. Try to make sure that you are still pressing the mat away and the shoulders are not collapsing. This is great for building your strength for handstands as well.

6. Pull Up Bent Elbow: This is a slightly advanced conditioning exercise. Once you have nailed a complete hammock pull-up, this should be your next step in building more shoulder strength. From a standing position with the hammock behind your shoulders, raise your arms and wrap your hands around the fabric twice. Breathe in to prepare and as you breathe out, pull up to come into a position where your elbows are completely bent, not halfway or partially but to a complete pull-up position. Hold this for 10 secs with normal breathing, feet pointed and the entire body in one straight line. Come down, relax and applaud yourself for a job well done!

P.S.: To start with, try to do 5 reps with pulling up and slowly coming down. Hold the pull up position for 10 seconds after the 5th rep. To challenge yourself further, in each of the 5 reps, try to hold the pull up position for 15-20 seconds and make sure the descent is always controlled.

7. Straddle Back: This exercise is absolutely crucial for your inversion strength and technique while being in the air. It develops strength in your lower abdominal muscles and helps you understand what it means to invert your entire lower body using your core strength and understanding how to tuck the pelvis under at the same time. The primary movements of the hip that are performed in this move are **flexion, abduction, and external rotation**.

Coordination is key to a clean straddle. To begin this exercise, lie down on your mat with your palms facing down right next to your hips, your pubic bone slightly tucked in towards your abdomen and your feet pointed. Breathe in to prepare and as you breathe out, lift your legs like you would in a shoulder stand but this time instead of making a straight line like a shoulder stand, simply take the legs over your head and the moment the feet cross the line of your forehead, open your legs in a clean straddle. Don't allow the chest to collapse. Think of keeping it alive and expanded throughout this set. While bringing the legs back down on the mat, keep the core really active to make sure that the legs don't just collapse onto the mat. Don't touch your feet on the mat and then carry on to complete the rest of the reps. 2 sets of 10 reps minimum. Maximum being your desire to invert in the air and it's equivalent in terms of reps! Now go slay!

Variation

Try straddles on the hammock after you have done them on the floor. Pull up and then invert to go into a straddle. It may seem challenging at first to invert with straight legs, so feel free to bend your knees in the beginning and then try the straddle with straight legs eventually. Keep practicing and adding golden feathers to your hat.

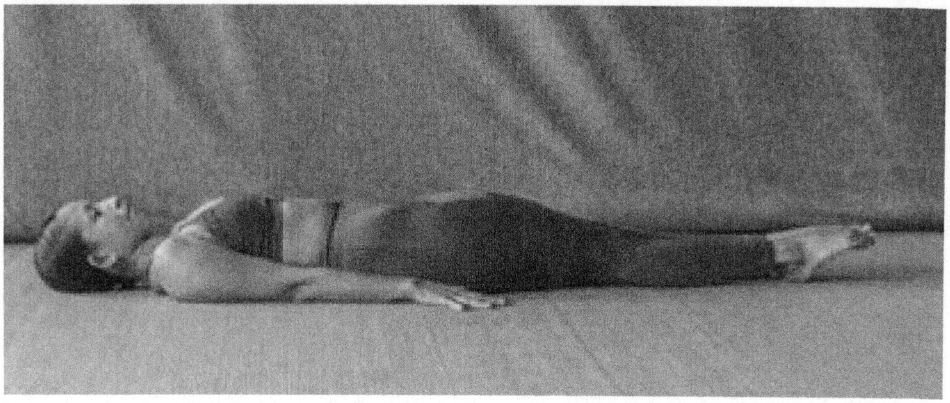

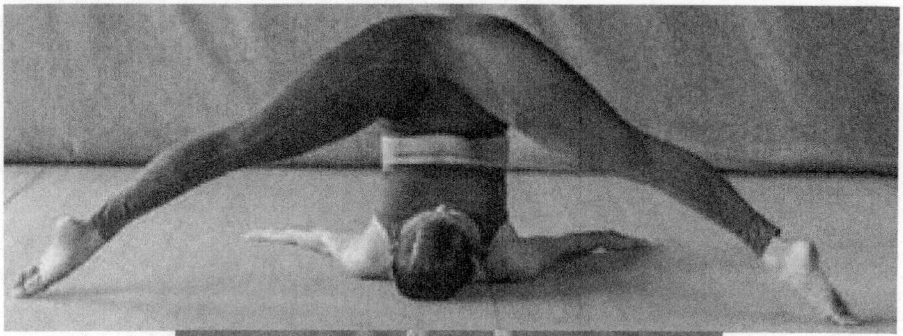

"

Studio Naach Stories

If we can do it, so can you

Anuradha Guglani is a very successful architect and artist based in Goa. She started her aerial journey at the age of 46 with a nagging back pain that refused to go over a period of years. Having suffered 2 slip discs over 10 years, her condition eventually became chronic with her being in and out of bed rest every 3 months. She started cycling and that really helped her but the fear to do anything intense remained with her. That is when she was introduced to Aerial Yoga and realized that she was able to develop core strength, upper body strength and flexibility without damaging anything and over the past 2 years of being consistent with aerial, she has almost forgotten that she lived 10 years of her life inactive due to the fear of getting an attack and feeling deprived. Round of applause for her dedication!

"

Chapter Eight

Basic Inversions

Let us now jump into the airborne world with an introduction to the basic inversions that can be done with a hammock. Once you taste this upside-down world, chances are the ordinary world might not entice you that much anymore! I don't blame you at all. I too love the airborne world a lot! Let's get started on understanding the nitty-gritties of this world. Just remember to practice all of these positions with a professional guiding you if you are starting your aerial journey. Not ideal to practice this alone if you are a complete beginner.

1. Hanging Sirsasana: The hanging sirsasana might seem daunting at first and you may even think that this is definitely not for you. But once you get in there and see how it makes you feel, I'm willing to bet that you will be thinking that this is definitely for you! And better still, what were you doing without it all this time?

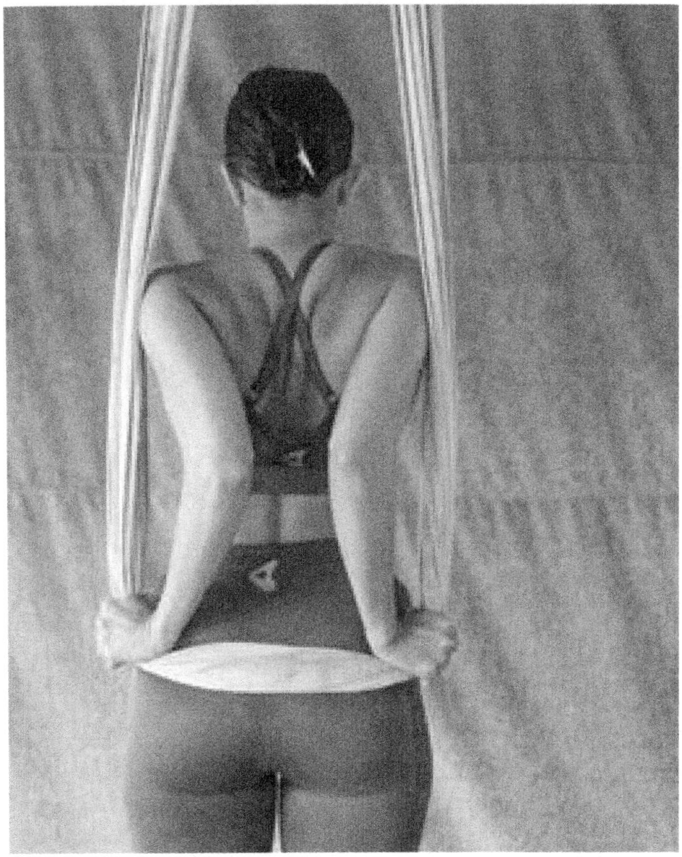

To begin with, while going into the sirsasana, remember that the hammock needs to be placed right on the sacrum area and it has to be maintained there as you are about to invert. If it goes higher up, it will cause discomfort from arching of the lower back and if you take it below your sacrum area, you wouldn't really be able to do much apart from sliding onto the floor.

Long story short, keep the hammock RIGHT behind the sacrum, take the support of your hands and hold the hammock hip-distance apart with your thumbs facing down. You want to ensure that your thumbs are wider than hip-distance so that when you invert, your thumbs don't get squished.

From there, maintain the position of the hammock, lean back and hug your knees to your chest. Open your knees into a butterfly pose immediately and slide your hands higher up the hammock keeping the elbows straight. This will give you a feeling of being on a swing and that is great! Allow your body to get acquainted with this sensation and once that is done, start sliding your fingers down the hammock and keep shifting your upper torso lower towards the full inversion by clipping your feet in front of the hammock in the same butterfly position. It will be quite effortless if you keep the body relaxed and breathing even. Once you are comfortably in the position, relax your arms by interlacing the elbows and just allowing the hammock to take your entire body weight.

Allow the lower back to relax completely and enjoy this pose where you can get lovely spinal traction and enjoy the benefits of inversion. Deep belly-breathing is ideal for this pose to go deeper into relaxation and allow the spine to lengthen.

This pose is great to stretch out the spine and decrease pressure on the discs and nerve roots. It may also increase the space between the vertebrae. Potential benefits of hanging upside down during inversion therapy include: short-term relief from back pain, sciatica, and scoliosis. Now isn't this just amazing?

Tips

- Make sure that the fabric is placed in the correct position
- Keep your thumbs wider than hip-distance so they don't get stuck under your hips as you invert
- Try not to push the floor with your hands or arch your back. Allow the hammock to take your weight and simply relax

2. Sarvangasana: Sarvangasana, also known as shoulder stand is called Sarvangasana because "sarvang" means all the limbs of the body, indicating that this asana uses all the parts of your body and has tremendous benefits for the entire system!

As you practice this asana, you might run the risk of feeling like a bat. That's okay. You are not alone in that. And let's face it, who doesn't want to feel like batman every now and then? You wouldn't be reading this book if it wasn't an exciting prospect in your mind already!

To get into the pose, you want to sit down inside the hammock with your feet still outside. Lean back and as you lean back, you might have to adjust yourself a little bit to make sure that your shoulders are completely covered with the fabric. At the same time, don't let the fabric gather too much because it will create discomfort in your neck in case the fabric digs in. Take just enough to make sure that the shoulders are supported. Once you have done that, hug your knees to your chest and grab the tips of the fabric on either side and slide your hands up till the elbows are straight. Place your feet right above your hands on the fabric. Flex your feet, prepare your body in the inhale and as you exhale, pull the fabric down and push the pelvis up by sliding your feet along the fabric till your body comes into a straight line.

Now you have successfully formed the posture to look like a bat. From there, you can still lightly hold the hammock with your fingertips or simply join your hands in namaste and enjoy this feeling. The hammock is completely supporting you.

Go into deep belly-breathing and relax the neck and allow it to just hang. To come out of it, simply bring your knees towards your chest, straighten both the legs and tumble into your mat. If the tumble variation seems too challenging in the beginning, you can simply sit back inside the hammock. Keep your head down for a few breaths as a lot of blood has rushed to your brain and your heart.

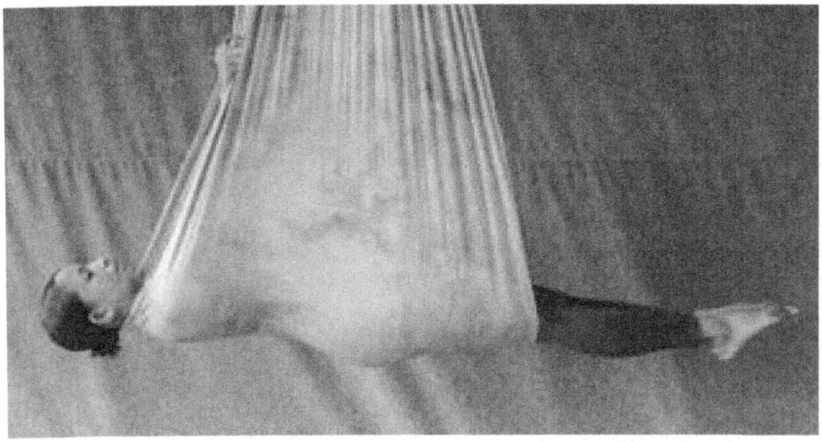

For a slightly more challenging variation, you can try Hanumanasana from Sarvangasana. Start gathering the entire fabric with your fingers. Once you have the entire bunch of the fabric in your fist, release the feet from the side of the fabric and bring them together with the heels and big toes touching each other. Keep the feet pointed and try to find a balance there for a few seconds. The pelvis may start sinking back and to avoid this, you should ensure that you are PULLING the fabric down and PUSHING the pelvis up keeping the Mula Bandha active.

From there, open the legs to go into a full Hanumanasana. Keeping the chest expanded will immensely help in going into a full Hanumanasana. Try both the sides and then you can tumble down to come out of the asana. Tumble down by bringing both the legs straight down towards the mat while keeping the abdomen tucked in.

Tips

- Pelvis should not sink
- Feet flexed and placed on the fabric
- Keep the chest expanded to reduce stress on neck
- Don't allow too much fabric to gather around your neck

Chapter Nine

Basic Moving Asanas

Before we start moving into the fully dynamic asanas and series on the hammock, it is crucial to have a great understanding of what it means to hold yourself while being in the air. Holding yourself strong while being in the air requires some amount of skill, patience and courage to try everything with a smile! With those ingredients, I am sure that you are a recipe for success!

So let's start with the 2 basic moving asanas-

1. Chair Pull-Ups with Hammock
2. Dandasana

1. Chair Pull-Ups / L-Tucks: For this series, you need to stand inside the hammock. Place your right foot inside the hammock, ensuring that the hammock is in the center arch of the foot. Slide both hands up on either side of the hammock and make sure that your hands are all the way up and the elbows are not bent. The standing leg (left leg) remains strong. In one shot, push the right foot down into the hammock as you pull yourself up to a standing position. Once there, bring your hands on either side of your shoulders.

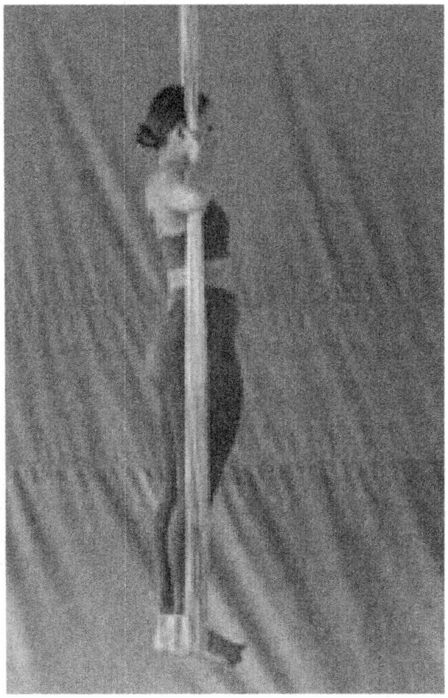

Now, maintaining it there, try to lead the movement with your hips and sink down towards your mat to come into an almost sitting position which is your L-tuck position. Keep the back of the knees straight as you slide into your L-tuck position. Without adjusting your hands, lead from the pelvis and push the hips back up to come to a standing position. Repeat this at least 5-6 times. To come out of it, just slide one foot out of the hammock, slide down by bending the other leg and step out of the hammock. Bravo! You have done it!

Tips

- Sink your glutes all the way down to come to the L-tuck position. Imagine almost coming to a full sitting position
- Lead with the pelvis to make the motion smoother while coming back to a standing position
- Don't allow the knees to bend when you slide your hips down for the L-tuck
- Keep breathing and enjoy the strength building in your shoulders
- Keep the feet active throughout by pressing them firmly against the hammock

2. Dandasana: This one is a super fun pose once you are in it. Come into a standing position inside the hammock. Once there, take your right hand inside and around the fabric on your right side. Grab the fabric with the thumb facing up. Now start rotating from your hips, turn your body to the right side till you get the fabric in the center of your glutes. From there, push the fabric with your left hand to make the elbow straight. Make sure that your left hand follows the line of your shoulder and don't place it too high or low. From there, take your left foot and place it at a slight height on the left fabric and push it away. Make sure that the left foot is turned out and not turned in and the fabric is behind the center arch of the foot. The left elbow remains straight throughout.

As you push with your foot, slide down with your hips till you come to a resting position on the hammock with one foot on top of the other. Once you have started sliding down, you can let go of the left hand (yes, you really can!) and bring it to the right side of the fabric above your head. Once seated, don't resist the fabric! Trust me, that won't feel comfortable! Surrender your body weight into it. Now slowly, yes slowly, trust yourself and let go of both the hands. Raise your arms above your shoulder level and make sure your arms are still visible from the periphery of your vision. Fix your gaze on your big toe or something small that is unmoving and just focus your attention on the air passing in and out of your nostrils. Observe it. It's the same breath that keeps you alive!

From there, bring your hands back over the top of your head and hold the fabric with both thumbs facing upward. Bring your head out from the left side, only the head. Breathe in and as you breathe out, pull the fabric down ensuring that both elbows are facing up and push the pelvis up. You want to ensure that the head remains thrown back and the glutes remain active as you are pushing the pelvis up. Repeat this 2-3 times. Then slide the head back in and come back to the same sitting position as before.

To come out of it, simply bend your knees and your hips will naturally slide down. Grab one side of the hammock and step out from the other side.

Tips

- Make sure to push the fabric away when you turn your hips and lift the leg up. Also ensure that the foot comes high, just under the fist
- When you are in a seated Dandasana pose, you will know that you are in the correct position if the feet and hips are in the same line. Try to avoid having the feet higher than the line of the hips and as you end up sinking too much towards the ground.
- Once you are in the Dandasana pose, allow the hammock to take your weight and don't keep the body too tight or the hammock may dig in. And don't forget to enjoy yourself!

Studio Naach Stories

If we can do it, so can you

Andrea D'Mello is a shipping and logistics consultant with over 20 years of experience in her field. She started aerial at age of 41 to jubilate her 42nd birthday with a bang. In her words, aerial has given her the strength and belief that only we can choose how high we want to soar! Her fluidity and grace have been a treat to watch and her consistency is an inspiration to all of us. A big round of applause for Andrea D' Mello!

Chapter Ten

Advanced Inversions

1. Upavistha Konasana Series
2. Double Sirsasana + Hasta Padangusthasana Series
3. Utthita Hasta Padangusthasana to Bhujangasana Series
4. Single Pigeon (Kapotasana) to Shalabhasana

1. Upavistha Konasana Series: The Upavistha Konasana series is a sequence starting from the hanging sirsasana. To begin with, start by going into a Sirsasana. Next, you want to straighten both your legs inside the hammock with the feet going around and up the fabric. As you hang upside down, push the floor with your arms and try to straighten the legs inside the hammock. Then bend the right knee and bring the fabric under the right knee. In one shot, inhale and as you exhale, reach for the fabric on the right side with the right hand. Reach so much that the right hand comes completely in line with the left foot. Then bend the left knee, bring the fabric behind the knee and reach for the fabric. Stay there for a few breaths to adjust yourself and bring the knees and the feet together. Make sure that your elbows are straight to ensure that no unnecessary tension starts building up in the shoulders and the feet are pointed.

For the next step, to go into Upavistha Konasana, you want to point your feet and straighten both the legs, keeping them together. Inhale, hold your breath, then on the sharp exhale, open your legs and come into the Upavistha Konasana. Try not to arch the back too much and relax deeper into it. Keep the length of the legs active and lengthened (back of the knees straight) to avoid the fabric digging too much into your skin. Next, slide your hands up the length of the fabric. Pull up with the hands and close the legs together in unison. The purpose of this is to slide the fabric closer to the groin area. Once there, the fabric fits comfortably on the skin. Arch your back by pushing the pelvis forward as you slide your elbows out of the fabric to come into a Dhanurasana or bow pose. You can arch depending on the level of your practice. To feel a deeper stretch here, you can slide your hands lower and that will immediately open the chest more. Keep the back of the knees straight and feet pointed with activation across the entire length of your legs.

To complete the series and come out of it, first marvel that you have come so far! After that, you want to let go of the left hand. Reach out with the left hand almost imagining that you are painting the area around you in a semi-circular motion and bend the right knee at the same time to turn and bring the body down. Your right knee clip should be strong and firm. You have successfully come into an inverted stag. Trust yourself and revel in this final position by letting go of both of your arms and finding balance while being airborne. To come out of it, lift your head and reach for the fabric on the left side with both hands, unclip the right leg and you are back to the ground! Repeat the same thing on the left side and don't forget to breathe! Again, make sure that you have somebody spotting you if you are trying this for the first time.

Note: It is absolutely normal to feel the fabric dig into your skin in the beginning. It takes a while to get used to the sensation and within a month of regular practice, all the discomfort vanishes. Consistency is the key!

2. Double Sirsasana + Hasta Padangusthasana Series: This pose, as the name suggests, is simply Sirsasana done twice. The regular practice of Sirsasana strengthens the spine, improves blood circulation, checks water retention, prevents infections, maintains hormonal balance, lubricates the reproductive passage, checks blood pressure, maintains emotional and mental balance. Wow, that's a lot of good things, right?

To get into this, first get into a single Sirsasana and repeat the Upavistha Konasana series till you reach the position just before Dhanurasana. When you reach this position, avoid going into Dhanurasana by keeping your shoulders behind the fabric and lean back with the upper torso. At the same time, open your legs to go into a straddle by pushing the fabric away with your hands. While getting into the second straddle, ensure that the fabric slides and comes exactly on top of the first layer of the fabric. If not, it might slip and then end up digging into your skin too much if it's in the upper thigh area and ouch! Let's avoid this please! Then take the legs around and up the fabric the second time.

Once you are securely in the double sirsasana, we will head towards the single knee hold. To get into this, begin by straightening the left leg completely inside the hammock. Bend the left knee and get the fabric securely clipped behind the knee. Once in that position, just ensure that the knee-clip is strong. From there, hold the right side of the fabric and unwrap the right leg from around the fabric twice. Bring the right leg right next to your ears to come into a complete inverted Hasta Padangusthasana. You can even take the leg back and open the chest by going into an inverted stag position and trying the foot hold variation.

To come out of it, look to your belly button, lift your torso and grab the right fabric with both hands. From here, you will do an unclip and clip motion with your left leg to slide down the hammock. Simply extend the left leg to release the fabric behind it once and then bend your knee again immediately. You will come closer to the ground with this motion, then do the same thing again the second time, your left leg will be free to come off the hammock and you will be in a standing position again. Make sure that your torso is up all through this motion of releasing the left leg.

3. Utthita Hasta Padangusthasana to Bhujangasana Series: This series is mentioned right after double sirsasana as it can be performed using the same transition. For this series, when you come to your second sirsasana preparation, climb up again and come up to an Upavistha Konasana. Basically, you will have a double wrap around your legs as opposed to a single wrap in a sirsasana. All through make sure that the entire length of your legs are very active and strong. Inactive legs cause the fabric to dig in more creating more discomfort. To get into the Utthita Hasta Padangusthasana from the Upavistha Konasana, bring both your hands on the right side of the fabric. From there, you have to take your upper torso outside the fabric, make half a circle with the leg by taking it through the center of the fabric and come to clip the fabric behind the right knee.

Try to move the entire body as one block, keep your core engaged and keep the hands close to each other. After clipping the fabric behind the right knee, you can now extend both your arms as your entire body is completely supported by the fabric, then extend the right leg and grab the right toe. You have successfully completed the Utthita Hasta Padangusthasana. From here, bring your hands on either side of the fabric, slightly pull up and bring your body to the right side and come into the dancers' pose. Find balance here with both the legs extended or one leg in **Passé** (a dance term in ballet where the knee is bent to create a triangular shape) and the other extended and both the arms outstretched behind the fabric.

To get into Bhujangasana, bring both hands on the right side of the fabric. Take the torso back and shoot the left leg between the fabric creating a full turn. By pushing the pelvis up and pulling the fabric down, you are in a full Bhujangasana! The fabric should come to rest right under the right shoulder, supporting you. You can keep your elbows bent to help you find stability in the pose. If you wish to challenge yourself further, you can try to extend and slide up the arms completely along the length of the fabric, making it a lot more challenging for your shoulders, back and chest.

To come out from the Bhujangasana, you want to reverse the entire flow. Hold the fabric which is under your right shoulder with both hands and then start turning towards your right side and get the left leg through the gap. Do this same motion 2 times and you will see yourself coming closer to the ground. Do the same motion a third time and you will end up in a clear inverted stag position. Clap for yourself! This wasn't an easy feat!

4. Single Pigeon (Kapotasana) to Shalabhasana: This one is one of my personal favorites and is extremely beneficial for lower ab strengthening, lower back and gluteal strengthening and of course shoulders and arm strengthening. To get into the Pigeon pose, first of all, we invert to get into a straddle with open legs. From there, we take legs inside and around the hammock (Just like Sirsasana). Bend the right knee and bring the fabric securely behind the knee while keeping the left leg still straight. Bring the left toes around the fabric securely. Keep them pushing against the fabric throughout or your foot might slip out.

Now bring both your hands on the right side of the fabric and start climbing up with the hands while pushing the fabric on the left side away. This motion has to be done in sync with each other. Climb with the right hand and push with the left foot. From here, bend the left knee and keep climbing from the right side and you will come securely in a Kapotasana. Make sure that the left toes are always active.

Precautionary note: Avoid Kapotasana if you have had any kind of knee injury, surgery or previous discomfort in the area around the knee. The inward rotation of the knee can be a little challenging and try this pose only after 4-5 months of regular aerial practice and guided training. You can try the tumble to Shalabhasana instead if you have had any history of knee pain.

To get into Shalabhasana from here, you want to push the fabric away with the left hand, release the left foot and slide back down bringing the knees and the feet together. Make sure that both the elbows are straight and the feet are pointed. Now, as you pull the fabric down, tuck in your legs towards your head to prepare for a tumble. Keep your chin tucked in till your legs go over your head and you flip your torso up to come into Shalabhasana. It is very important to keep the grip of the hands strong and not let them slide down as you tumble back. Once you have reached the position, mentally applaud yourself, then let the left hand go and bend the right knee to come into the inverted stag. Repeat the same thing on the left side and you are a maestro with the Pigeon Series!

"

Studio Naach Stories

If we can do it, so can you

Malika Ahluwalia is a painter and creative soul for whom Aerial was love at first sight! She was never very keen on traditional yoga but found the combination of Hatha and Aerial together extremely exciting and totally up to her alley! She started Aerial at the age of 29 and feels that Aerial makes her feel strong yet extremely light. She continues to raise the vibrations of the class with her sense of humor, wit and intelligence. A big round of applause for Malika Ahluwalia!

"

Chapter Eleven
Advanced Moving Asanas

1. Sagittarius
2. Double Pigeon to Hip Key
3. Angel Balance
4. Merry Go Round
5. Crossback Straddle to Needle

1. Sagittarius: Sagittarius is an advanced pose and it may take some time for the body to understand it. That's fine. To be awesome, one needs to be patient. Well, let's get started, shall we?

1. Step into the hammock by placing one foot on the hammock. Make sure that the knee goes inside the hammock and your hands slide up the hammock to hold it. Make sure that you reach as high as possible ensuring straight elbows.
2. Push the foot inside the hammock to stand up and bring the other foot right next to it. Keep your hands next to your shoulders.
3. Take your right foot outside the hammock (foot pointed) and then around it to create a loop around the foot.
4. Slide the right foot up the fabric, then push the fabric away from your body and shift your body weight entirely to the left side by taking the left leg off the fabric. Laterally rotate the left hip so that the fabric is resting and supporting

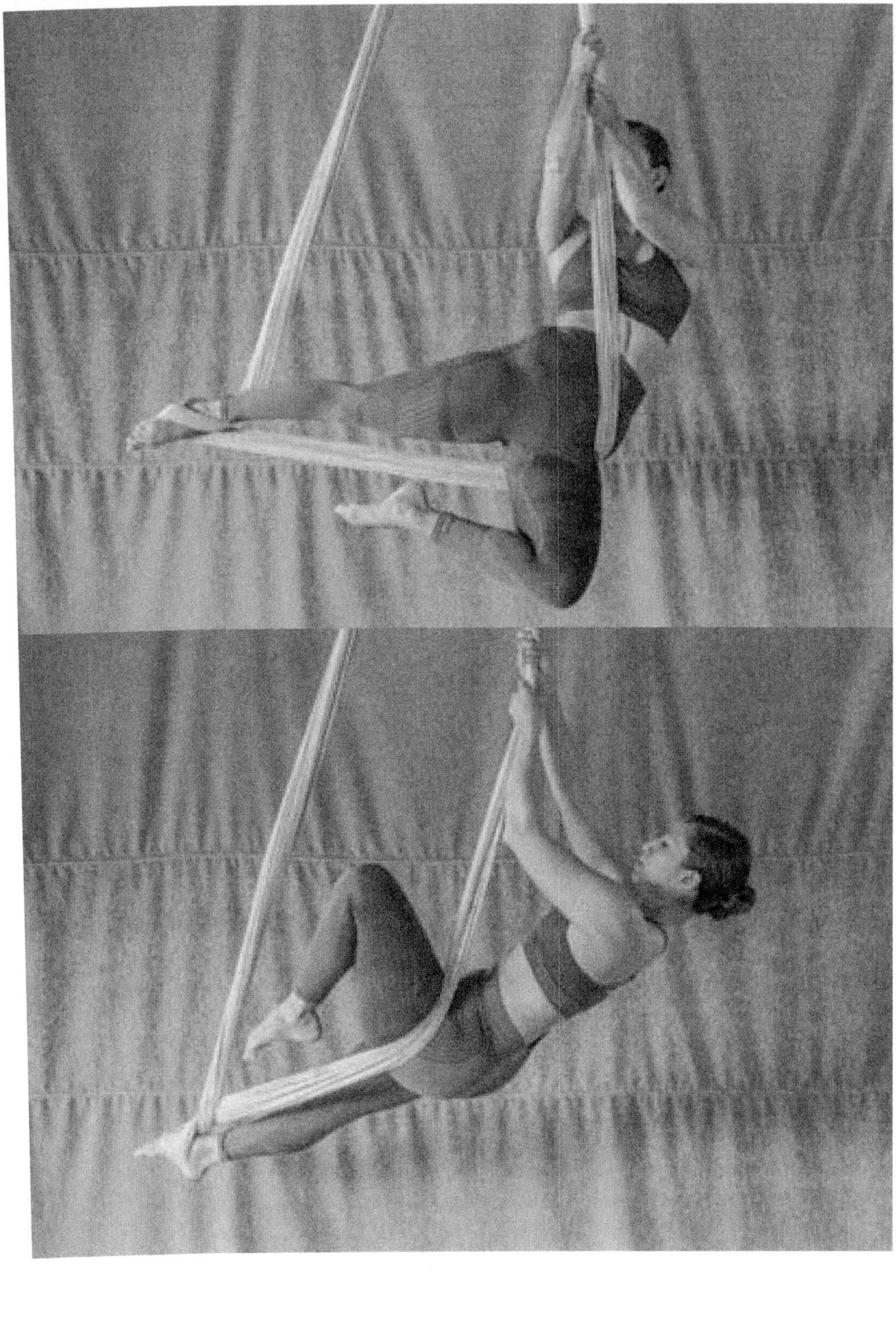

the left hip completely. From there, bring both your arms to the left side of the fabric. Extend the right arm all the way straight up the fabric and let go of the left hand to find a nice shape and a moment of pause before you start preparing for the turns.

5. Make sure the left foot is pointed and the back of the knee is straight. Also ensure that the right foot, knee and hip are in a straight line, pushing the fabric away to avoid any kind of knee discomfort.
6. Find the alignment of the left arm and left leg. Keep the right arm straight.
7. Bring both hands close to each other and hold the fabric with a strong grip. Make sure that the right leg is super active with the foot consciously pushing the fabric away.
8. Bend the left knee to come into a passe position (A dance term where the foot of one leg comes close to the knee of the other leg to create a triangular shape)
9. Keep the abdomen strong and don't allow the back to arch. We will go into a round of 3 full turns.
10. Turn towards your LEFT shoulder and as you turn make sure to bring the knee back INSIDE the fabric
11. Turn 3 times to complete the Sagittarius. Make sure to travel up the fabric with your hands on each turn. You can turn 1 or 2 times also in the beginning. It's okay. We love you anyway.
12. You should come back to the exact position as when you had just started Sagittarius with your left leg, left arm in one line.
13. To come out of the final Sagittarius pose, reverse the entire motion done so far by bringing the torso out from the left side of the fabric and turning in the opposite direction with the left leg (basically towards your left big toe). You will come back to a neutral standing position and applaud yourself for having come so far!

Tips

- Be extremely aware that while you are turning, the leg pushing the fabric away does not bend at all. If it bends, you are allowing a crunch to happen in your obliques which could lead to a tad painful muscle spasm. Lengthening your entire body is of key importance. Start with a single turn or two turns since the sensation of the fabric on your foot might be a new one and could take time to get used to

- To start the turns, always turn TOWARDS the pinkie toe of the extended leg and to come out of it, always turn towards the big toe
- When you push the fabric away to shift your weight to the left side, you need to ensure that you slide the right foot as high up as possible to create more space between the 2 poles of the fabric. The more space you have, the easier it will be to turn

Happy turning!

2. Double Pigeon: Double Pigeon or the Stallion is a majestic pose created in the hammock which deeply stretches the lower abdomen, hips, psoas, groin, pelvis and hamstrings. The preparation is the same as Sagittarius. It requires a basic understanding of managing your body weight during an inversion and keeping the entire body active throughout. There are many wonderful variations that can be done from this position. Now let's get started for Double Pigeon-

1. Start the double pigeon series by coming into a standing position on the hammock.
2. Point your right foot and raise the leg to 45 degrees. Take it outside the hammock and then wrap it around the fabric to create a loop around the foot.
3. Slide the right foot up the fabric, then push the fabric away from your body and shift your body weight entirely to the left side by taking the left leg off the fabric. Laterally rotate the left hip so that the fabric is resting and supporting the left hip completely. From there, bring both your arms to the left side of the fabric. Extend the right arm all the way straight up the fabric and let go of the left hand to find a nice shape and a moment of pause before you start preparing for double pigeon.
4. Make sure the left foot is pointed and the back of the knee is straight. So far, the preparation is identical to Sagittarius and it will change from here on.
5. Keeping both your hands on the left side of the fabric, turn the right hip to change the positioning of the fabric and the orientation of the right leg. Earlier your toes were pointing forward and now they will point upwards. The fabric should be touching the outside of your right thigh while supporting your lower back completely. You are basically pulling up slightly to shift the fabric into a more secure and supported position for the next step.
6. Lean back now while your right foot is still active and come into a straddle. You need to make sure that the fabric is in the right place to come into a secure straddle.

7. Now hold the left fabric with both hands and clip the left knee on the fabric. Make sure that the fabric does not slip out from the supporting position behind your back. For this to happen, keep the glutes pushing outwards until you have a stable clip on the fabric.

8. Keeping both hands on the left side of the fabric, climb up to gracefully come into a double pigeon. While coming up, get your right hand on the right side of the fabric and come up with control.
9. Once there, throw your head back and push the fabric away with your left arm keeping the elbow straight.
10. To come out of it, slide your hands up the fabric and you can make the body straight again by pulling the fabric down to come to a standing position.

11. This will create a fabric lock on your left thigh. You may want the lock to be as high as possible.
12. Now, change the grip of your hands by bringing the right arm on the left side of the fabric above your head and the left hand right under the lock on your thigh. Keeping the grip strong, release the right foot from the fabric and turn your entire body towards the left side to come into a hip key. Once you are in

the hip key, let go of the bottom hand and you will slide into a neat drop on the fabric.

13. Lean back again to free your leg and you have successfully completed your double pigeon!

Tips:

- In the hip key, make sure that the fabric is under your hip bone and the upper torso and lower torso are coming towards each other. You can practice this from a lower height before trying it from the double pigeon sequence
- Keep the glutes pushing down towards the ground while preparing to go into a straddle. That is crucial to ensure that you don't fall out of the fabric
- Keep the right leg very active and firmly pushing the fabric away while the left leg is bent

3. Angel Balance: This pose is a complete beauty. Yes, it does make you feel like a flying angel or just a superhero basically. It's the closest you get to Wonder-Woman or Superman. Take your pick and let's get started-

1. To get into the pose, first, come to a standing position inside the hammock.
2. From here, raise your right hand and bring it inside the hammock next to your thigh.
3. Wrap the right wrist and hand around the fabric and do the same thing on the left side.
4. Push your glutes back so that the hands and elbows have ample space to get the right grip.

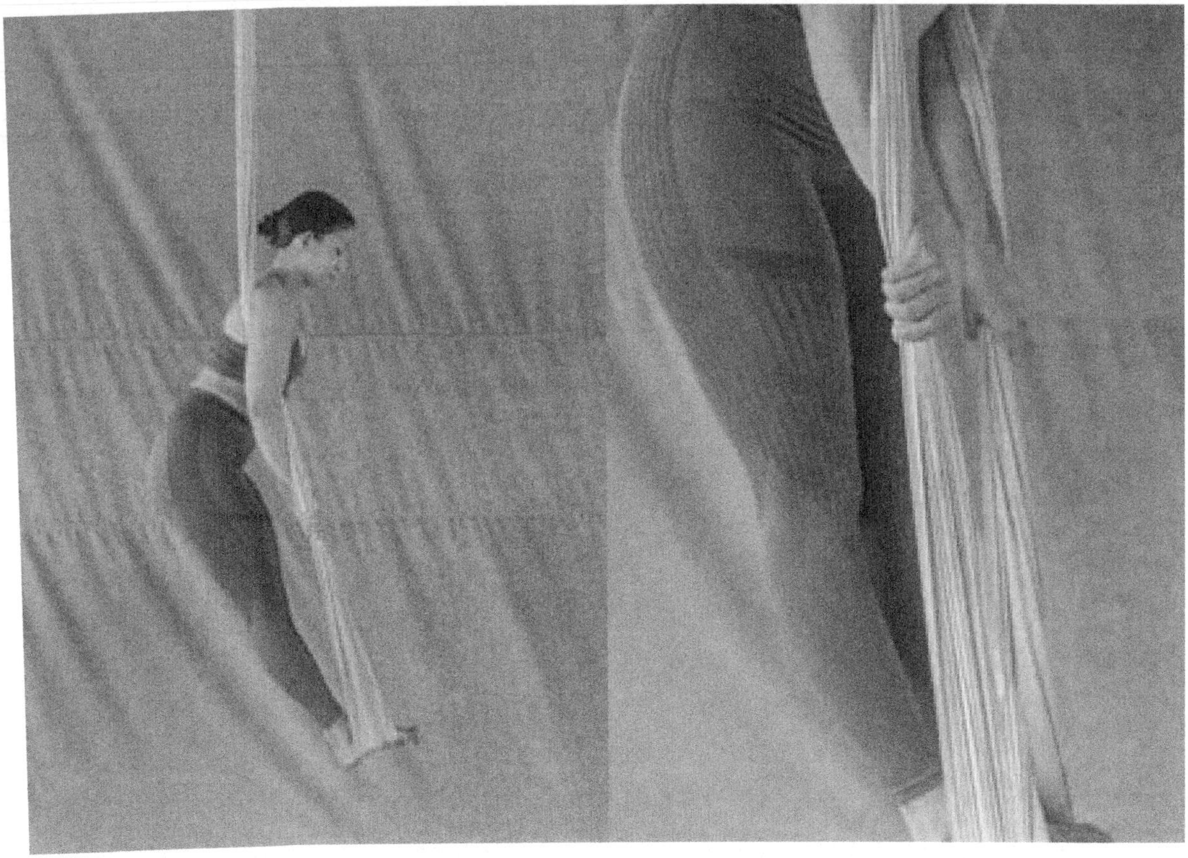

5. If your elbows are still bent, you are not in the right position. It will place too much stress on your wrists. Lean back enough to make sure that the grip is strong with straight elbows.
6. Once you feel strong in your grip, roll the shoulders back and make sure they are not rolling forward into a hunch. Chest expansion is key.
7. Start by removing one foot at a time to test the strength of your grip.
8. Ideally, once you have a strong grip, hug both knees to your chest and take them behind the fabric.
9. Make sure the shoulders are not collapsing as you hold the pose.
10. The legs should be in an arch line and not ahead of the hips
11. Keep the glutes active and you can even throw your head back to get more expansion from the chest.

12. To come out of it, step back into the hammock with both feet. Slide one hand up with the thumb facing up, the same thing on the other side, just slide down by taking one leg out and step out of it.

Good job there!

4. Merry Go Round: We call this one Merry Go Round as we end up turning around quite a few times and who doesn't love Merry Go Round anyway? So let's start turning, shall we?

1. For this flow, you need to open the fabric wide and place the entire length of your right leg inside the hammock. Your foot should come out from the other end. Basically, the fabric is covering your inner thigh to your ankle.
2. If your right leg is inside the hammock, your hands should be grabbing the left side of the fabric. Make sure that both your hands are reaching as high as possible. The elbows should be straight.

3. From here, slightly bend the right knee outward inside the hammock. Lean back, keep the hands where they are and then take the left leg inside the fabric from the gap creating a full circle. Come to the lotus pose by pushing the fabric away and crossing the left leg over the right.

4. Then shift your hands slightly further up, bring your torso back towards the fabric in front of you, then repeat another turn and find balance in the arabesque pose. You can lock your neck on one side of the fabric and let both hands go or keep holding the fabric with one hand if it makes you feel more secure.
5. You can stay here and enjoy this pose for a while and then head for the knee-hang in inverted stag pose. As you can see, an inverted stag is being used as a transition pose in this particular sequence.

6. For the knee-hang, take half a turn more and bring the upper body outside the hammock
7. As you do this, bend the right knee to get the fabric right under your knee. Make sure that your knee clip (grip from the back of the knee) is very strong.
8. Depending on how comfortable you feel with the strength of your knee clip, you can either let go of both hands and grab your ankle or hold the fabric with one hand and grab your ankle with the other.

9. Depending on how comfortable you feel with the strength of your knee clip, you can either let go of both hands and grab your ankle or hold the fabric with one hand and grab your ankle with the other.
10. To come back, grab the loose fabric again and do the twin motion of straightening your right leg and bringing your torso back inside the hammock.
11. To come out of it, untwist 2 times by kicking your left leg twice, come to a comfortable gomukhasana by crossing your free leg over the hammock and locking your left elbow. Repeat the same step on the other side and you are definitely becoming a Merry Go Round!

Tips

- While doing the first turn, ensure that the left leg does not touch the fabric at all. If it does, the fabric will immediately gather, dig into your skin and you won't be able to perform the second turn which would be a shame, right?

- While kicking/turning with the left leg, think of pushing your pelvis up each time you turn and take your hands up the fabric simultaneously with the turn of the leg. This will ensure smooth turns and you will have enough space to take the leg through the fabric
- Keep the back of the knees straight while kicking the left leg and make sure you warm up the hamstrings well to ensure this happens

5. Cross-Back Straddle to Natarajasana: This sequence is quite challenging yet fun to do. Try this once you have clean inversions on the floor and the air. All the straddles that you practiced on your mat will come into play now! Let's get started!

1. Come into a standing position inside the hammock.
2. Take your right leg behind the hammock and open it slightly to get the fabric resting and supporting your right inner thigh.
3. Slide your right hand and shoulder outside the fabric.
4. Do the same thing with your head and your left shoulder as well.
5. Your entire body weight is now on the right side of the hammock.

6. Bring both your hands right next to your right shoulder and take a full turn towards your right shoulder.
7. As you turn, squeeze your glutes and push the hips forward to reach out with your right arm.
8. Now grab the left side of the fabric with your left hand, making sure that the left shoulder is still outside the hammock.
9. Open the right and the left leg simultaneously to create a cross in your back. Ta-da! That's why it's called Cross-Back Straddle. Pull up to get the cross securely on your lower back.

10. Now you need to invert your upper body and open your legs at the same time. Initially, when this seems hard, you can start by doing it one by one. First only open the legs and then push the fabric with your hands to come into a full straddle with open legs. Think of this as an Inverted Upavistha Konasana. Let both hands go and revel in this upside down magic. You are successfully in the Cross-Back Straddle!
11. From here, to prepare for the needle pose, wrap your right leg around the right side of the fabric while making sure that the left leg is still straight.
12. Bring both hands right above the left leg near your torso and take your left leg through the gap. Keep the back of the knees straight.

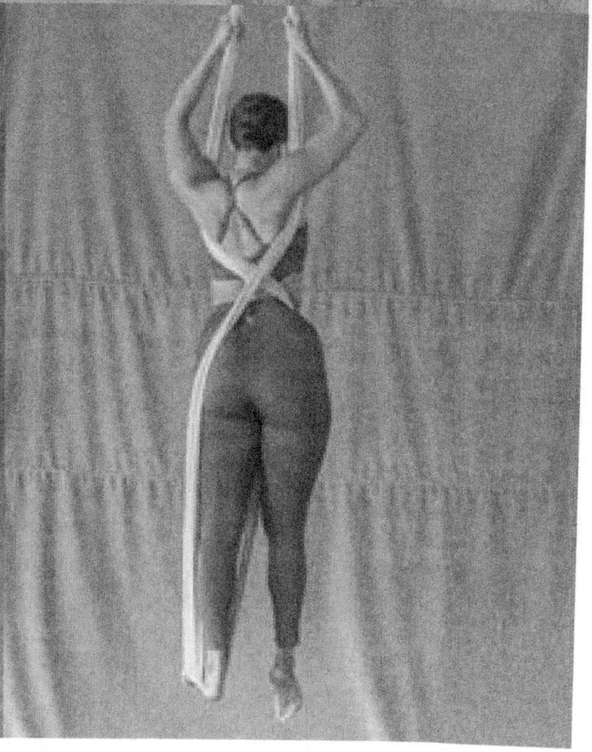

13. As you turn, let go of your right hand and take it around to grab the fabric behind your lower back. Once you do that, let go of the left and bring it on top of the right hand. Raise your torso and bring it inside the fabric. Note that both the hip points are facing the front at this moment.
14. From here, push the fabric away and rotate the right hip to close it towards the fabric while pushing the fabric away with your hands. Keep the elbows straight and hands apart from each other with one hand above the other. Make sure that both hands have a sufficient amount of distance from each other to keep the stability of your pose.
15. You have successfully completed your Natarajasana pose!
16. To come out of it, open your hip again with both the hip points facing the front and take your right arm up the fabric, bring your torso inside the fabric and wrap your left hand below as well.

17. From here, gently release the top foot. Make sure that the obliques are engaged and the core is active while you are freeing the top foot to ensure that the leg comes down with control.
18. Your right leg will naturally come next to your left leg. Squeeze your inner thighs and keep the shoulders active to come into a sideward angel balance pose. From here, you can simply slide down with your hands to step on the ground and you have successfully completed the Natarajasana Series!

Tips

- Practice this pose safely and make sure you do not try it if you are a complete beginner
- This sequence requires good hip and shoulder flexibility along with core stability and you can surely get there with dedicated practice
- Keep the legs straight while inverting into a straddle

Chapter Twelve

Precautions While Practicing Aerial

Here are a few things to keep in mind while teaching Aerial:

1. You will, for sure, have students that may be trying inversions for the first time in their lives. Some will be thrilled to try and some will be very scared. Always be around a student who has come for the first time, especially during inversions because you want to ensure that they feel safe and supported.
2. Whenever you are teaching something advanced, please make sure that you have one person spotting the other. This will make certain that no one is trying anything new and challenging unchaperoned. Any kind of fall can be damaging both mentally and physically. But if we stand for each other, every mistake or fall becomes a chance to share and grow together.
3. Learning things upside-down can be disorienting. So it is always a great idea to explain things step-by-step and break it down into parts so that it's not too much information for people to take.
4. Always find out the history of your students. People with Vertigo, heart issues, high blood pressure or lower back injuries need special care or maybe should opt for restoration over a full blown aerial class. Make sure you always do a thorough background check.
5. Never miss conditioning on the floor before you start the moving series inside the hammock. Pull-ups, ab work, straddles are all extremely essential to feel strong and safe while doing the more advanced asanas on the hammock.
6. If you are trying anything from the advanced moving asanas flow, please make sure that you have a crash mat under you and again, always have a professional spotting a new student.
7. Last but not the least, never forget to have fun! Aerial can be extremely fun and can become addictive; this is the best part about it! Make sure the environment is full of love, fun and support and your students will surely love to fly!

With this, we come to the end of this beautiful flying journey. Take care of your bodies, take care of your minds and enjoy your practice. It has genuinely been a joy to share the journey of Aerial Flow Yoga with you and I just want you to know, again and again, that if I can do it, so can you.

I have had people from all walks of life, all shapes and sizes walk into my class. I have been amazed to see the potential of the human body and have seen myths relating to age, ability, body type, core strength and ability, all bust in front of my eyes. With the right direction, a supportive environment and precise training, the joy of training is real and it is waiting for you as you read this book. Go make it happen! I thank each and everyone who has made this aerial journey such a memorable one and I hope your journey is amazing too. I believe in you!

Printed in Great Britain
by Amazon

73824359R00099